D1752158

The Little Book of Why

Written by
Catherine Ann Russell

Illustrated by
Morgan Grace Quist Sooy

The Little Book of Why by Catherine Ann Russell

Hardcover ISBN: 978-1-956693-12-6
Paperback ISBN: 978-1-956693-13-3
eBook ISBN: 978-1-956693-14-0

Library of Congress Number: 2022900315

The Little Book of Why, Second Edition © 2022 Catherine Ann Russell
First Edition Printing, 2019 BookBaby Self-Publishing (hardcover only)

Printed in the United States of America

All rights reserved. This book, or any portion thereof, may not be reproduced or used in any manner whatsoever without the express written permission of the publisher except for the use of brief quotations in a book review.

Basketful Relief Project
POB 994
Lyons, CO 80540
cat@basketfulreliefproject.com

The Little Book of Why is a children's picture book written for the Basketful Relief Project (BRP) dedicated to help fund emergency famine relief efforts around the world. The BRP donates gift dollars to established relief organizations from the purchase of this book. To find out more visit: www.basketfulreliefproject.com.

Copyediting by Katie Chambers of Beacon Point Services (beaconpointservices.org)

Cover and interior design by Janell E. Robisch of Speculations Editing (speculationsediting.com)

Illustrations by Morgan Grace Quist Sooy

To my dad, John, and my sister, Emily,

With love.

Over the hills, in a land not far from you, there lived a little girl named Belle and her father, Ben. Now Ben loved his daughter very much, and they would often take long walks through the hills and valleys near their home, with Belle lifted high upon his shoulders.

Here on this lofty perch, Belle could see all that there was to see. It was a beautiful February day, a time when winter is touched by the hints of an upcoming spring.

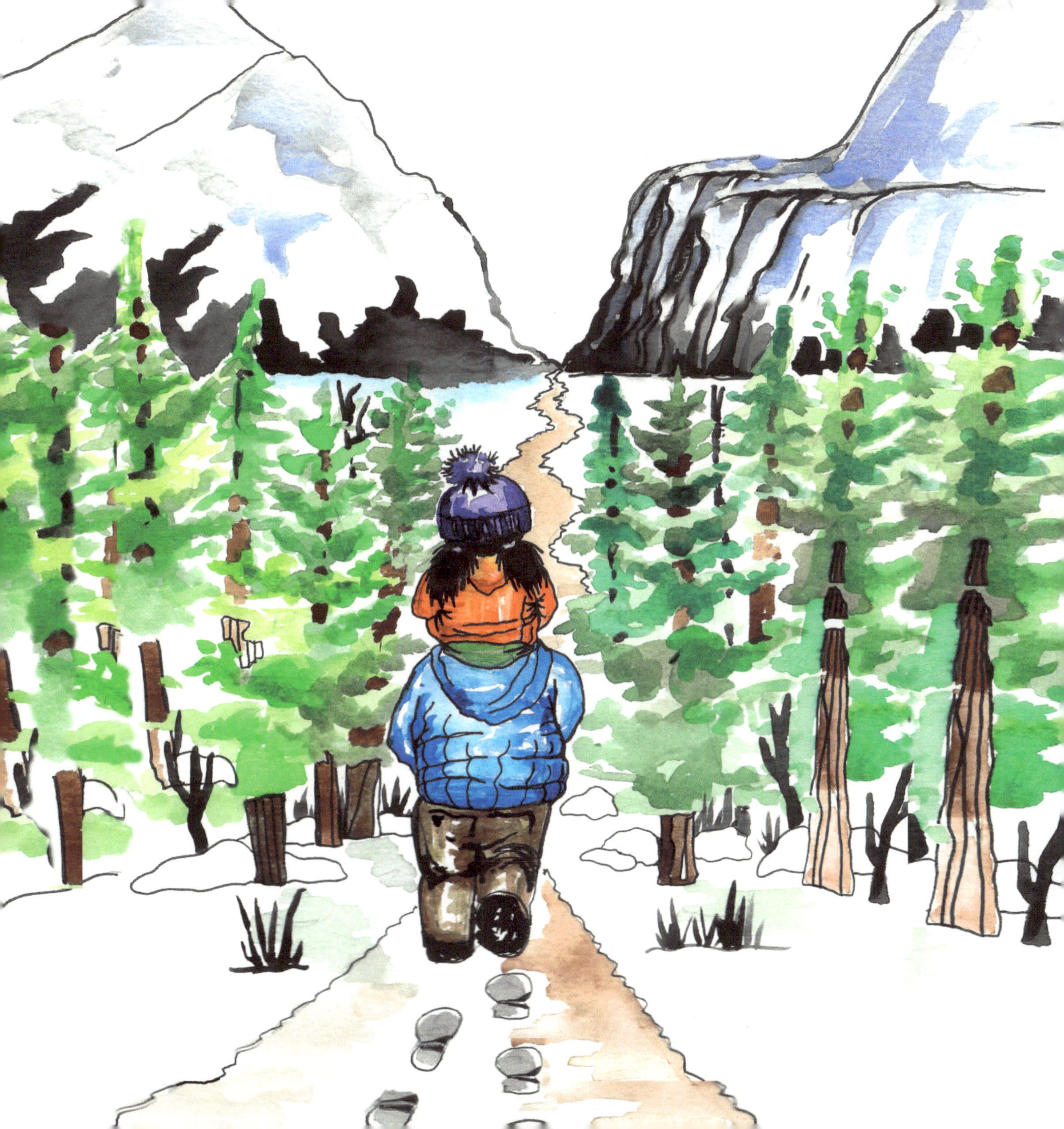

On this walk, they spotted magpies making mischief in a nearby tree,

A deer on the hillside,

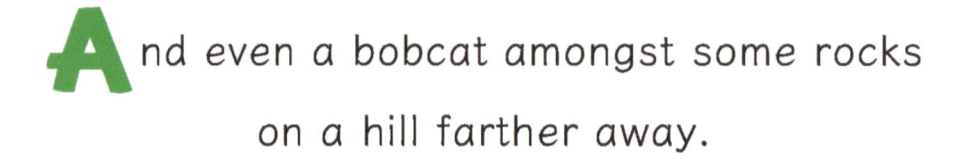

And even a bobcat amongst some rocks on a hill farther away.

It was a wonderful time together and all felt right in the world.

Soon Belle and Ben came upon a beautiful frozen lake. Belle gazed at the sight before her, wide-eyed. After Ben set her down beside him, she noticed an open puddle of water right at their feet.

Belle looked at the frozen lake and then at the puddle, and being a deep thinker and very inquisitive, she asked,

"Papa, why is the water frozen out there but melted right at our feet?"

"Ah, Belle," her father replied, "this is because the water is shallower here at our feet than in the middle of the lake, so it can warm up and melt faster than out there."

Belle thought on this long and hard as they both sat down to relax by the frozen lake. Then she asked,

"Why does shallow water heat up faster than deep water?"

"Do the fish in the lake like the frozen deep part or the warmer shallow part?"

"Do fish freeze in the lake in the winter?"

"And what kinds of fish are in this lake, anyway?"

By this time, Ben had lifted Belle onto his shoulders and had wisely decided to move on from the lake, for the day was beautiful and all felt right in the world.

High on top of her father's shoulders, Belle took in the world around her.

She gazed at the mountain cliffs and the cascading wind-driven snow.

She marveled at a gigantic pine tree,

And a water-barren riverbed that would soon be a torrent of spring melt from the snowpack above.

Then she asked,

"Papa, why are there deer in the world?"

"And bobcats?"

"And birds?"

"And mountain cliffs with snow?"

"And huge trees?"

"And frozen lakes in winter?"

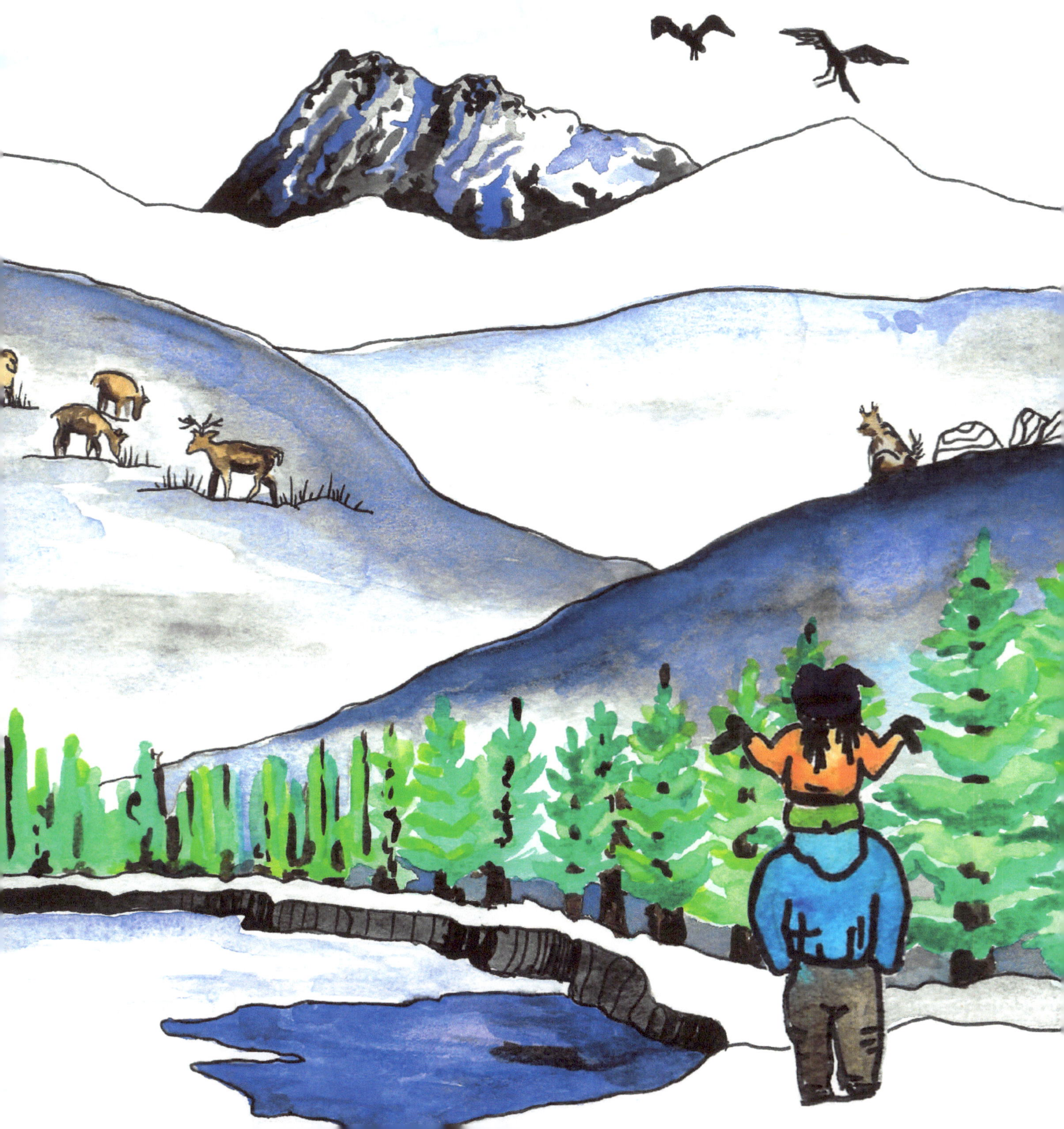

Ben furrowed his brow and felt a little trickle of perspiration down his cheek. Belle's questions were getting tougher. He imagined a large report card with the letter grade slipping from a perfect A. But before he could answer, Belle had already moved on, for on this beautiful February day, Belle was on a roll.

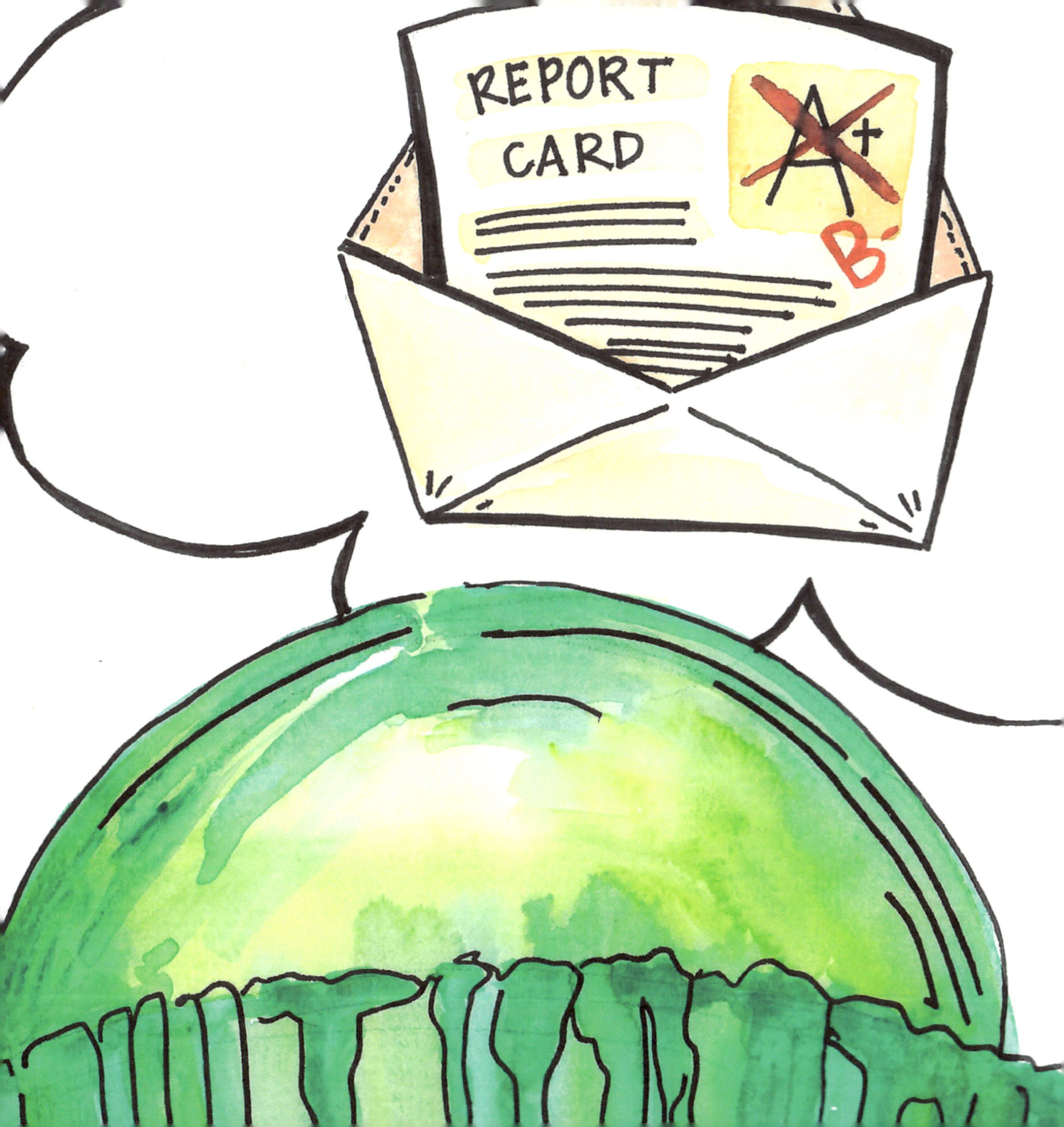
REPORT CARD
A+
B-

"Papa, who planted all of the pine trees?"

"How long did it take for all these trees to grow?"

"Do pine trees get cold in winter like I do?"

"Why are the trees so tall and I'm short?"

Ben thought long and hard about these things as they crunched through the snow towards home. Belle kept asking questions, not bothered that her father was not answering. To Belle, it was a beautiful winter day and all felt right in the world.

As they approached their house in the open meadow, Ben chuckled to himself when Belle spied the chicken coop at the side of the house and asked,

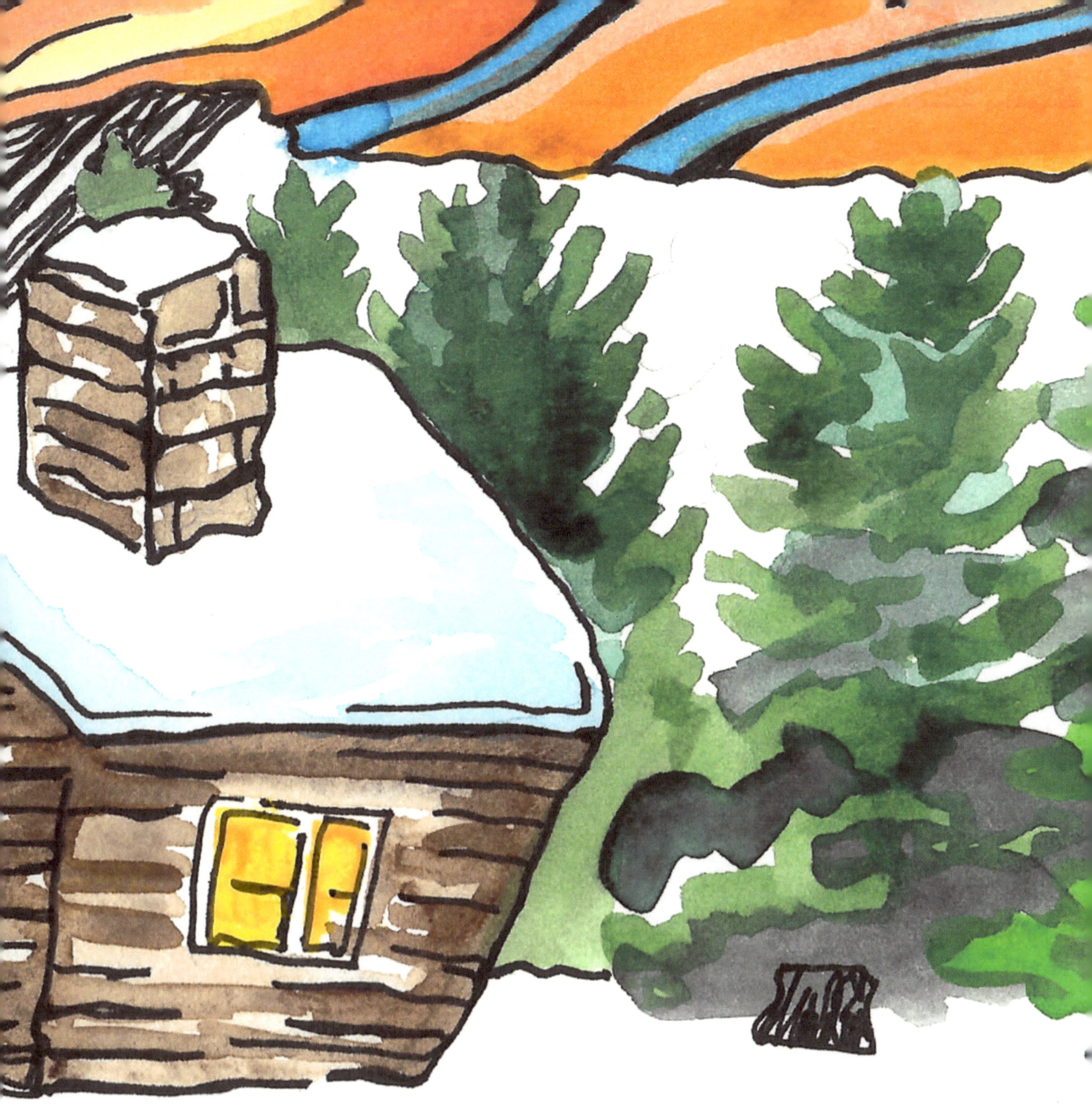

"Papa, which one came first, the chicken or the egg, and why?"

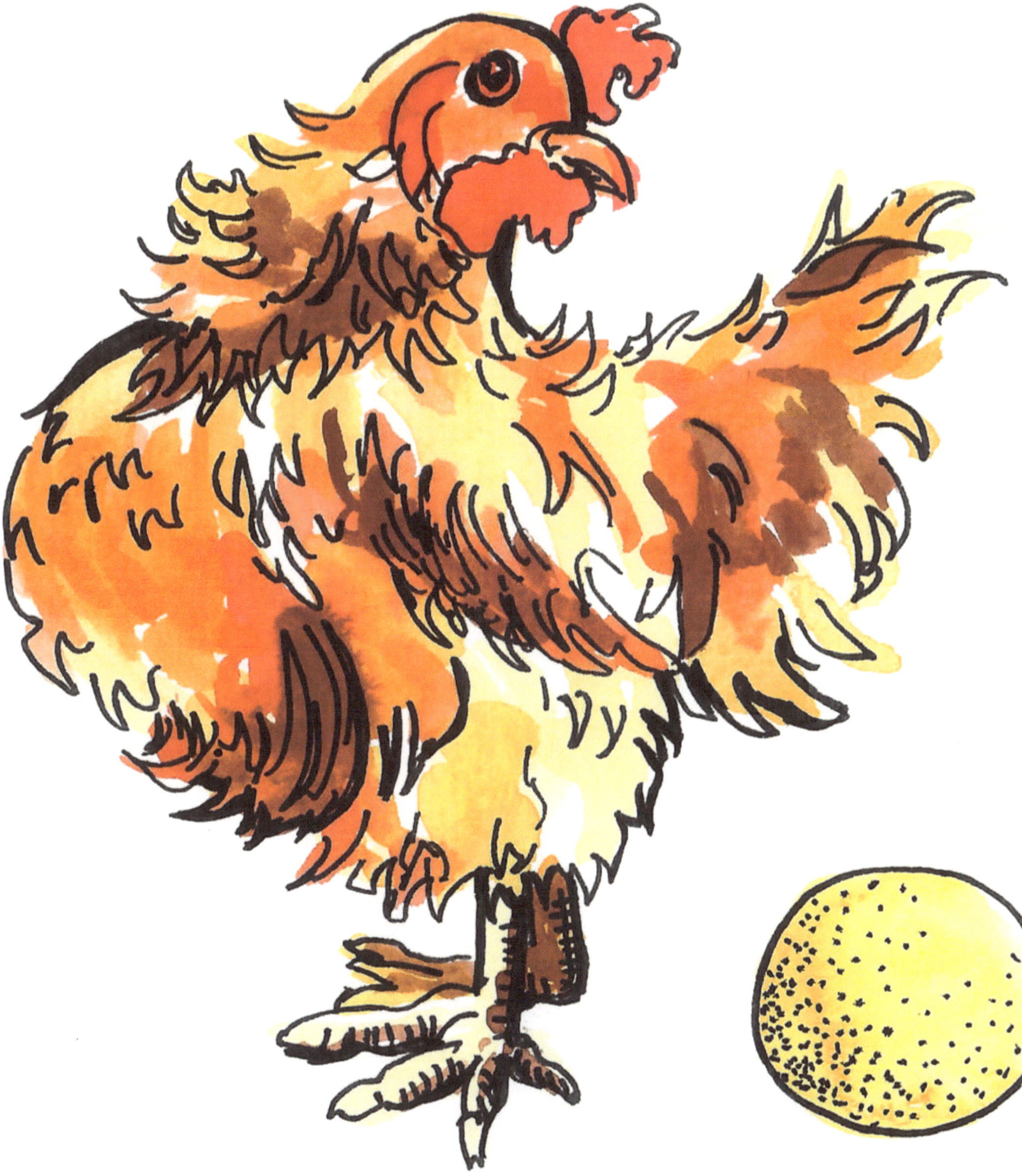

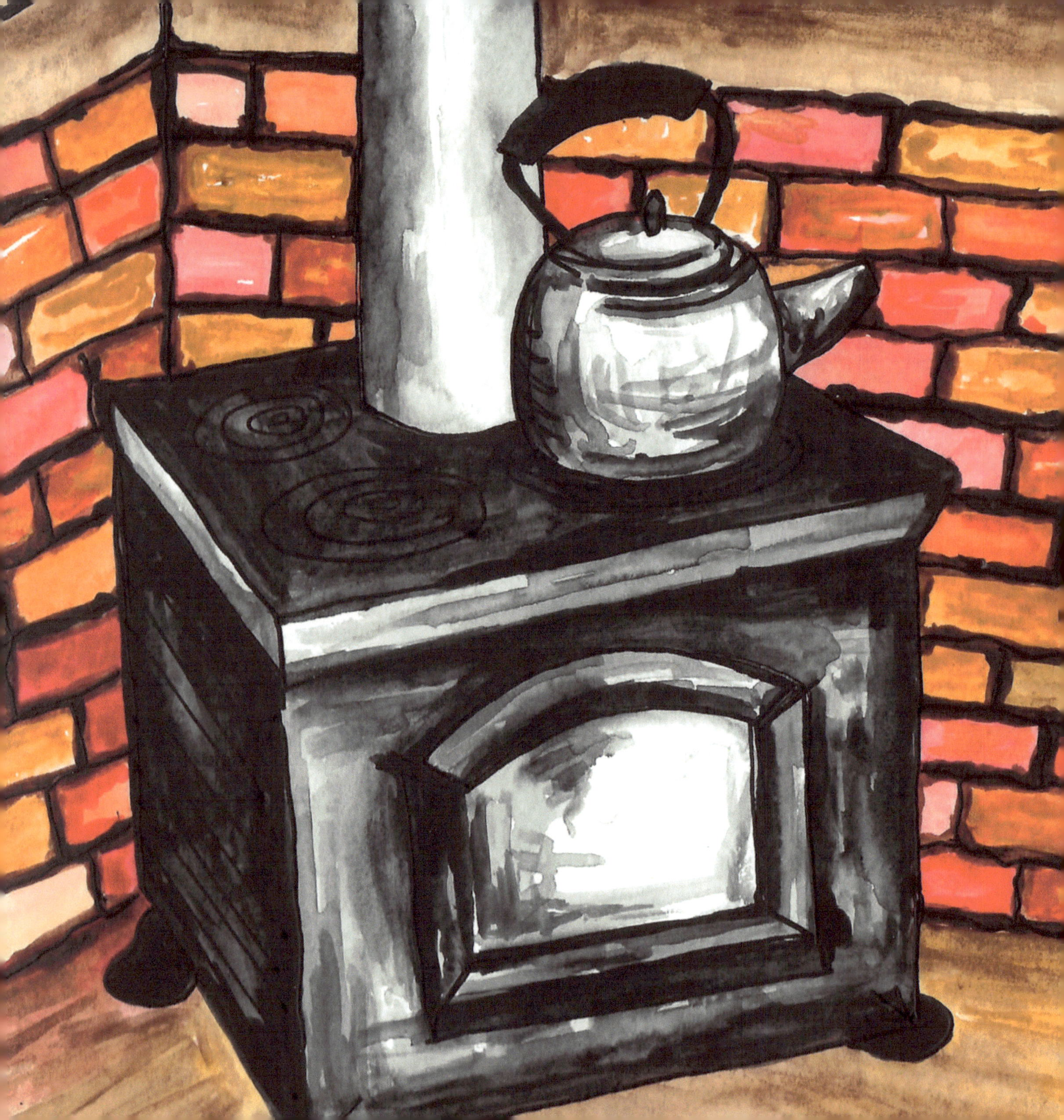

Father Ben's chuckle grew to a laugh as he scooped Belle up in his arms and carried her inside their little house. The full day together outdoors had made him giddy with delight. He busied himself firing up the kettle for some hot chocolate. As he watched her remove her boots, still chatting and asking questions, Ben, like Belle, felt all was right in the world.

That evening, Ben was tucking Belle into bed when she asked,

"Papa, why do you love me?"

"Ah, Belle"—Ben kissed her forehead—"that will take a lifetime to answer."

Belle thought long and hard on this until she fell fast asleep.

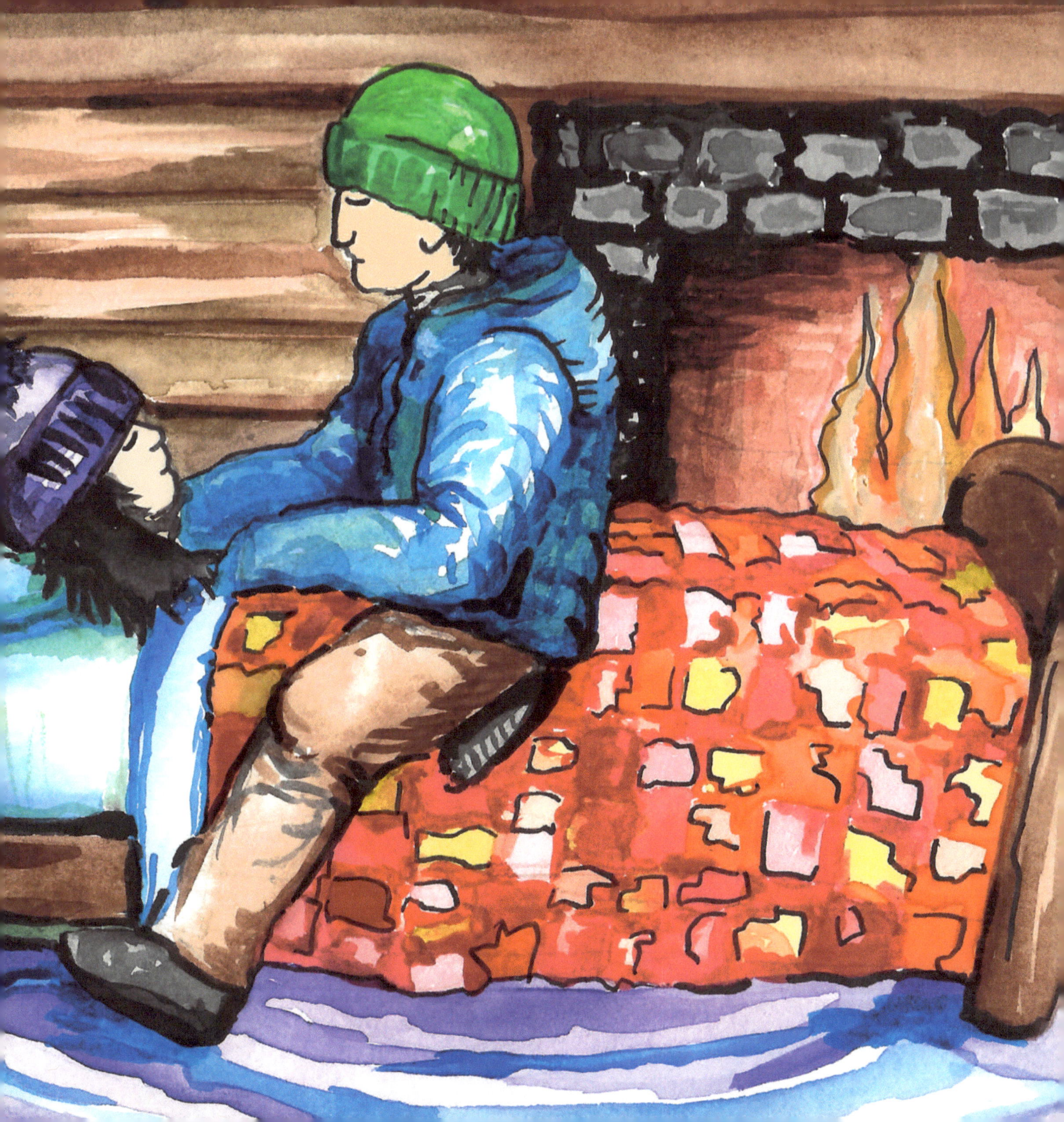

Meanwhile, Ben stepped outside, gazed up at a heaven full of stars, and pondered all of Belle's questions.

He sighed, feeling wonderfully, joyfully alive . . . but was not completely certain as to why.

ACKNOWLEDGEMENTS

Special thanks to:

Illustrator Morgan Grace Quist Sooy, who somehow managed time to lavish her talent on this fun children's book during many exciting life changes. Editor Katie Chambers of Beacon Point LLC, whose professional eye polished this work and made it shine. You have been a fun teacher and a life saver. Thanks also to proofreader Leona Skene of Intuitive Editing and designer Janell E. Robisch of Speculations Editing. You are each superb professionals as well as super fun to work with. Finally, I would like to thank the many energetic and savvy mentors at Self-Publishing School, without whom I would be lost at sea, navigating the daunting writing, marketing, and publishing world.

An author might have an inspiration for a story, but it takes a professional village to publish a successful book.

ABOUT THE AUTHOR & ILLUSTRATOR

Author Catherine (Cat) Ann Russell

Catherine (Cat) Ann Russell loves animals and nature very much. She lives with her husband, Ed, on a small farm in Lyons, Colorado, and has goats, chickens, ducks, and two cute burros named Nikki and Norman. At one time, Catherine had seven large Nubian goats, and she would take them all on a walk up the valley near her home. People in the neighborhood used to call her, "the goat lady." Before this time on the farm, Catherine worked many years as a scientist to study the sky and air. She released many weather balloons from canyons, fields, and even ships out at sea. People then used to call her "the balloon lady." Now, Catherine enjoys writing beautiful children's books. She hopes she can help feed little babies and children around the world by selling her books and donating money to organizations who care for children. She very much hopes one day people will call her "the book lady." You can find Catherine online at basketfulreliefproject.com and [spikeproductions.com.](spikeproductions.com)

Illustrator Morgan Grace Quist Sooy

Morgan Grace Quist is a nurse and artist who lives in the mountains of Colorado. She grew up adventuring in the outdoors: kayaking down rivers, pitching tents in the woods, climbing tall mountains, and catching lizards on the trails. The beauty of the natural world heavily influences her artistic pieces, and you'll often find her lost in the Colorado landscape with a paintbrush in hand.

BOOKS BY CATHERINE ANN RUSSELL

Basketful Relief Project (BRP)

Children's Picture Books

Get to Bed!
The Little Book of Why
Picco and Wren Three

Children's Chapter Books

The Pearls of Wisdom Series: Stories Inspired by a Biblical Proverb

Book 1: *The Pond of Reflection*
Book 2: *The Hyrax Song*
Book 3: *The Zoe-Chai Seed*

All books available soon in various formats by the end of the year, 2021 and 2022.

THANK YOU FOR READING
The Little Book of Why

I sincerely appreciate your feedback, and I love hearing what you have to say. Your input will make my future books better.

Please take two minutes to leave a helpful review on Amazon and/or GoodReads:

Basketfulreliefproject.com/book-reviews-the-little-book-of-why-2nd-ed/

Sincerely,
Catherine

CPSIA information can be obtained
at www.ICGtesting.com
Printed in the USA
BVHW011832231222
654908BV00010B/840